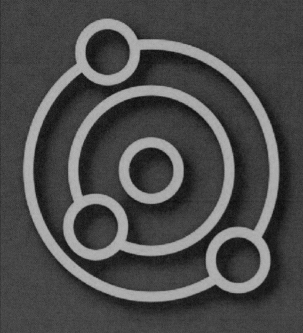

Physics

Chemistry

Math

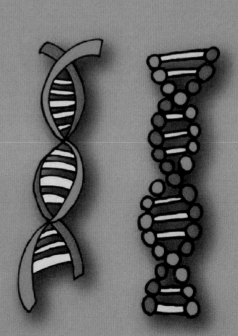

Biology

Atom

Electron

Force

Motion

Skull

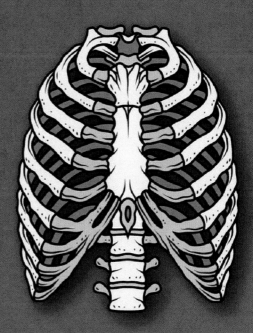

Ribes

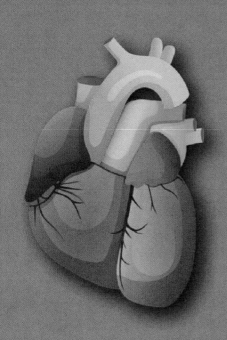

Heart

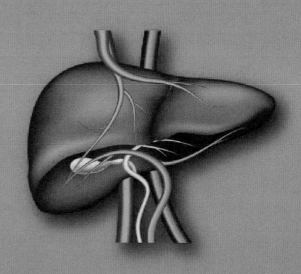

Liver

Earthquake

Electricity

Environment

Cloud

Cold

Brain

Heat

Air

Flood

Fossil

Matter

Migrate

Measure

Move

Observe

Plant

Day

Night

Weather

Tornado

Water

Thunderstorm

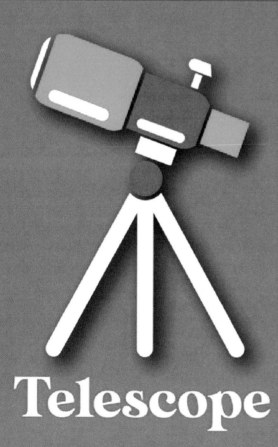

Telescope

Technology

Sun

Moon

Star

Speed

Space

Solar System

Soil

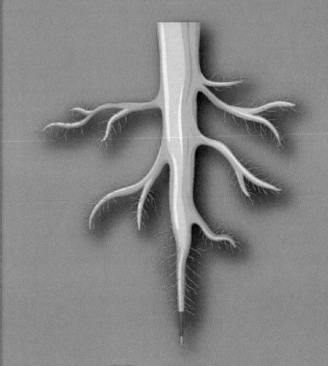

Root

River

Ocean

Pond

Lakes

Orbit

Hear

Gravity

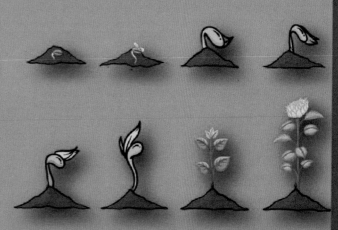

Germinate

Insect

Larva

Leaf

Life eycle

Tree

Recycle

Reduce

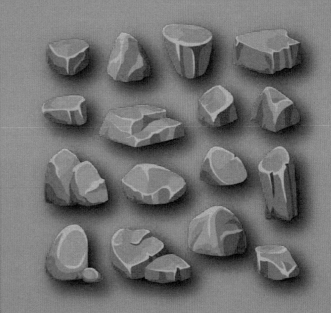

Rock

Rainbow

Temperature

Barometer

Earth

Lightning

Liquid

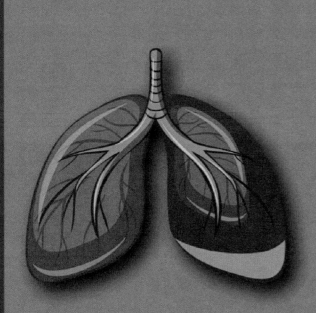

Lungs

Magnet

Satellite

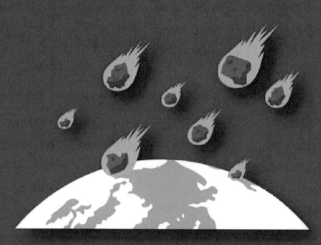

Meteor

Rocket

Venus

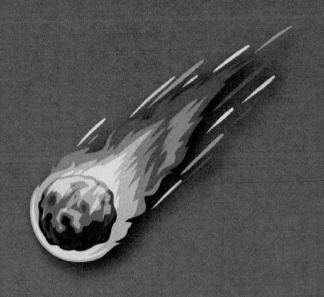

Asteroids

Mars

Cave

Hills

Island

Volcano

Compass

Spin

Push

Slide

Light

Mass

Prism

Switch

Plug

Battery

Fruit

Reflect

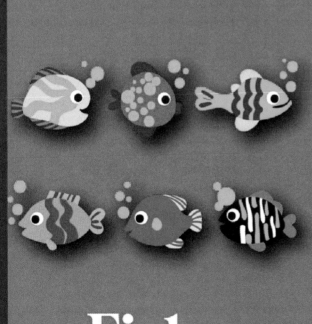

Fish

Meat

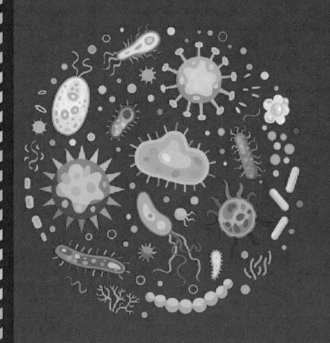

Bacteria

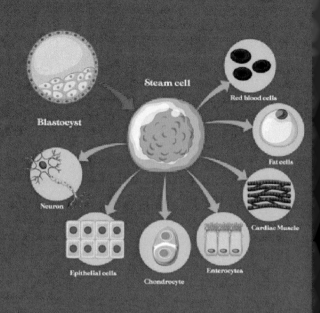

Cell

Bone

Birds

Magnify

Snow

Wave

Rainforest

Made in the USA
Las Vegas, NV
06 January 2025

15938271R00017